WELCOME TO THE JUNGLE

A coloring book for everyone
about changing wildlife habitats

by Ken Habarta

Second Edition
International Standard Book Number
ISBN: 978-1-9865-9214-7

Manufactured in the United States | 2018

A note from the Author

Welcome to the Jungle is an all-ages coloring book that depicts wildlife living and coping in an urbanized world. Seeing animals outside their natural habitats is often startling and points to more serious issues: humanity's fragile, precarious position in nature and mankind's responsibility to protect the Earth.

While environmental consciousness is higher than ever, our ever-expanding human footprint continues to pose dangers to the global ecosystem. This book serves not only to highlight the impact we have on the world around us, but also to continue raising consciousness for preserving natural habitats.

Proceeds from the sales of *Welcome to the Jungle* go to organizations helping protect and advocate for the future of wildlife.

There are many alligators that inhabit the Buffalo Creek Golf Course in Palmetto, Florida, but the giant, 15-foot-gator that saunters across the fairway is now a mascot of sorts for the players. Chubbs, as the gator is known, may look like a monster, but the club believes as long as its patrons continue to leave the reptile alone, golfers and gators can peacefully coexist.

A mountain lion showed its climbing prowess by scaling a 35-foot utility pole in the California desert. The animal apparently was frightened by some type of human activity and sought safety in the heights above. In an effort to coax the lion down from his perch, wardens asked passersby to continue onward and not stop to view the unusual spectacle. However, the lion apparently didn't feel safe enough to return to the earth before darkness fell.

A herd of buffalo somehow got loose and wandered around the upscale neighborhood of Pikesville Maryland, disrupting traffic and alarming homeowners before officers managed to corral them in a tennis court.

A wild coyote was spotted roaming around the roof of a bar in Long Island City, Queens in New York City. The coyote stayed there for more than an hour before it fled into an abandoned paint factory.

Three deer walk across San Francisco's iconic Golden Gate Bridge in California, holding up the evening rush hour traffic. The deer were first reported around 5:24 p.m., but once police officers arrived they were already gone.

A moose took a dip in a private swimming pool at a holiday villa in Redmond, Washington. The moose swam a few lengths of the pool before resting in the shallow end. The enormous animal managed to gracefully climb out, carefully stepping over the poolside deck chairs as it made an effort not to crush anything, and exited the area.

Zebras run down the city streets in the Belgian capital of Brussels. The animals escaped from a local zebra ranch and led police on a chase through the city until they were captured.

The wild turkey population took off about a decade ago in the more suburban neighborhoods of cities. Since then, the birds have become increasingly comfortable making their way into busier areas of the city. Wildlife can thrive when they have four things: the right food, water, shelter and space.

Toronto, Canada, is the self-proclaimed "raccoon capital of the world" and has been unable to outwit some of the city's cleverest "trash pandas." Even without thumbs, raccoons have nimble paws. Additionally, urban raccoons boast serious street smarts. One study by a raccoon expert revealed that raccoons knew to avoid busy intersections, and another study found that city raccoons are better than their country counterparts at figuring out how to open garbage can lids.

A gaggle of geese make their way through an industrial parking lot. Geese are good at choosing nesting sites, even if sometimes these sites are hard for us to understand. Canadian geese like open, flat spaces where they can see predators coming from far away, so parking lots look like great nesting spots.

Thousands of wild boars call Berlin home, where they dig up gardens, cause road accidents and openly move through neighbourhoods. Boars usually live on the outskirts of Berlin, but lately they've been coming more frequently toward the center. There are regular reports of joggers and dog-walkers encountering the beasts that can move their bulky bodies at 25 miles an hour.

As black bear numbers increase in some North American communities and more people move into bear habitat, encounters between bears and people have risen. Bears have a keen ability to detect pet food, garbage, barbecue grills and bird feeders—and once they locate a food source, they remember where it is.

About 100 escaped goats munched on manicured lawns in Idaho's capital city of Boise before being rounded up and hauled away. The owner of We Rent Goats said the 118 goats were grazing at a
nearby retention pond when they broke through a fence and went exploring.

A racoon scaled a 25-story office tower in Minneapolis before being safely trapped and released back into the wild. The raccoon apparently got itself stranded on a ledge of the Town Square office building in downtown St. Paul, likely on an errant mission to raid pigeon nests on the skyway over 7th Street.

Foxes in urban areas may be changing their behaviour to adapt to city life. As they are adaptable creatures and can flourish in built-up areas, cities represent a big conveyor belt of food that feeds all the things that foxes are eating.

As rabbit rural populations decline, new urban ones are growing. Rabbits are adapting to cities finding abundant nooks and crannies for shelter, sleeping and raising families.

Chacha, a male chimpanzee, fended off captors at Yagiyama Zoological Park after making a bid for freedom along electricity lines. The chimpanzee was on the loose for nearly two hours after it disappeared from the park in Sendai, Japan. The chimp had managed to climb over the wall of its enclosure before darting up a telephone pole and making a getaway on power lines. The primate managed to get 250 meters from the zoo before being hit with a sedative arrow and plunging from the wires into a blanket held by workers.

A man gestures to a hippopotamus at a flooded street in Tbilisi, Georgia. Floodwaters destroyed
enclosures at the zoo, killing some animals and letting loose others. The hippo was cornered in one
of the city's main squares and subdued with a tranquilizer gun.

A female peacock on the loose in a liquor store led an animal control officer on a chase that also led
to smashing bottles of wine and champagne before the bird was finally nabbed. The peahen walked
through an open door at the Royal Oaks Liquor Store in Arcadia, California, and made herself
at home in the liquor store. The peacock was eventually caught after spending 90 minutes in the
store and causing over $500 in damage.

A cow roams the highway after a tractor-trailer hauling cattle overturned near Atlanta, Georgia. The local transportation office captured a few of the cows that escaped from the tractor, but are still looking for more with the help of local authorities.

Welcome to the Jungle is part of Coloring for Change, a coloring book initative designed to create awareness, stimulate conversation and fund organizations focused on global issues.

Ken Habarta is a visual artist living in New York City and the Berkshires, Massacusetts. He also runs Big Cardinal, a strategic consultantcy helping companies navigate consumer culture.

Special thanks to everyone who helped make this book possible.

P.S. Please tweet photos of completed pictures on twitter with hashtag #welcometothejungle